► 2012 LONDON

INSIDE

RYAN LOCHTE

Fast and furious! "This is my time," says the Olympian, as he challenges Michael Phelps to be No. 1 in the world

► **AGE** 27 ► GAINESVILLE, FL

SWIMMING

"I don't pay much attention to what people say about me breaking records," Lochte tells *Us*. But he does admit, "I did Google myself — once!"

Bitter rivals? Hardly. "Win or lose, we're still going to be friends," says Lochte (with Phelps).

F rom the moment he straps on his goggles, all Ryan Lochte sees is the finish line. ★ ★ ★ ★ "Once I step foot on those blocks, something changes in me," the swimming sensation tells *Us*. "I'm no longer that laid-back person who likes to hang out with my teammates. I'm a racer, and I want to win." It's because of this tunnel vision — and his new strongman training! — that the six-time medalist has become a threat to longtime pal Michael Phelps. "I'm tossing beer kegs, lifting big tires," says Lochte, who plans to compete through the 2016 Games in Rio de Janeiro. "All that heavier weight lifting started after Beijing. I've just gotten so much faster, stronger and bigger since then."

No doubt, building up that überfit physique has helped in many ways. Chief among them: He's become one of the Olympics' most eligible bachelors! "The other guys don't like to talk about it, but I do think swimmers have the best bodies," he jokes. Another plus? This hunk wears his heart on his sleeve. "It's not that I don't have time to date. I just haven't found The One." In fact, he'll do just about anything for a lady with a killer smile: "Like, have you seen those movies where a guy sees a girl and their eyes lock, then the guy walks into a wall? Well, I did that once on purpose!" he confesses to *Us*. "Honestly, it worked. She ran over, asked if I was all right, we started talking and then we went on a date!"

"I'm a mama's boy!" gushes the star athlete (with mom Ileana, a day care director).

RYAN'S MOM REVEALS ALL

Mother knows best: Ileana, a former swim coach, taught her son how to power through the pool when he was just 5 years old. These days? "I travel with him wherever he goes," she tells *Us*. "I get more nervous than him at meets!"

What was Ryan like growing up?
He was a troublemaker! My parents and my sisters always feared what Ryan was going to do when I'd bring him over: whom he was going to kick or push, what he would break. We would hide little toys where he couldn't reach them, but he would always find a way to get up on the shelves.

How do you keep him grounded now?
I think it's all him. I really believe that he feels swimming doesn't define him. It's not the person he is. He's even lost track of where his medals are!

Has he treated you to any splurges?
His college diploma from the University of Florida was the biggest thing. *He* didn't care about finishing, but he knew it was important to me.

Mini mischief! "He'd play in our neighbors' yards," recalls his mom.

Lochte got his tough side from Mom. "Oh, gosh, I'm *very* competitive," admits Ileana.

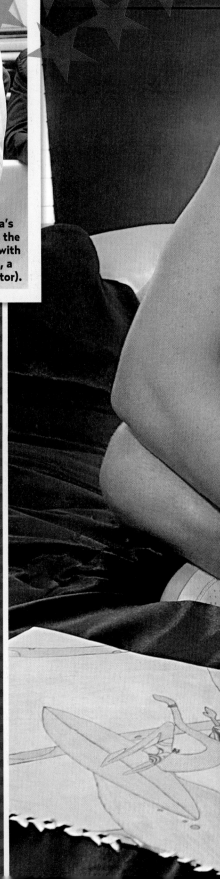

He describes his art as "kind of trippy," but says his more serious sketches involve fashion. "I want to design my own business suits and swimming apparel!"

SWIMMING

► **AGE** 27 ► BALTIMORE

MICHAEL
PHELPS

*The Olympic golden god opens up to Us about his
roller-coaster race to London and swimming his final lap*

Still proud of her boy! "It's heartwarming to watch Michael compete and carry himself as a young man," mom Debbie tells *Us*.

With Miss California ex Nicole Johnson, 27, an on-off flame since 2008.

Phelps admits he rarely wears his medals. Rather, he likes to keep them wrapped in an old T-shirt and stored in a makeup case!

A fter 20 years in the pool and 16 Olympic medals, Phelps knew he'd be slipping on his Speedo for the last time in London. "All I've known is this sport," he tells *Us*. "I always said I didn't want to swim past the age of 30." Yet deciding to retire was hardly simple. "There were times I just wouldn't come to practice," he admits. "It didn't excite me anymore." Indeed, he fell disastrously from grace after his historic eight gold medal wins in 2008. Not only did he blow off his coach in favor of Las Vegas trips, he earned a reputation for womanizing (among his flings: a cocktail waitress, a pageant queen and reality star Brittny Gastineau). He even got suspended for three months from the sport after being caught smoking marijuana — a moment he calls "the lowest point in my career."

But by 2010, he decided to clean up his act. "A number of things kicked in," he tells *Us*. For one: knowing only three medals kept him from the title of most decorated Olympian of all time. On top of that, teammate Ryan Lochte reignited his competitive fire after beating him (twice!) at last year's World Championships. "We like to joke around and have a good time," Phelps says. "But when I step up behind the block, I know only one person is going to win the race." Even more than reaching the finish line, however, Phelps can't wait for what lies beyond it. "I want to travel because I've been to so many amazing cities, but only seen the pools. *That's* what I'm looking forward to: going to Rio de Janeiro in 2016 to cheer on my country and see what it's like on the other side."

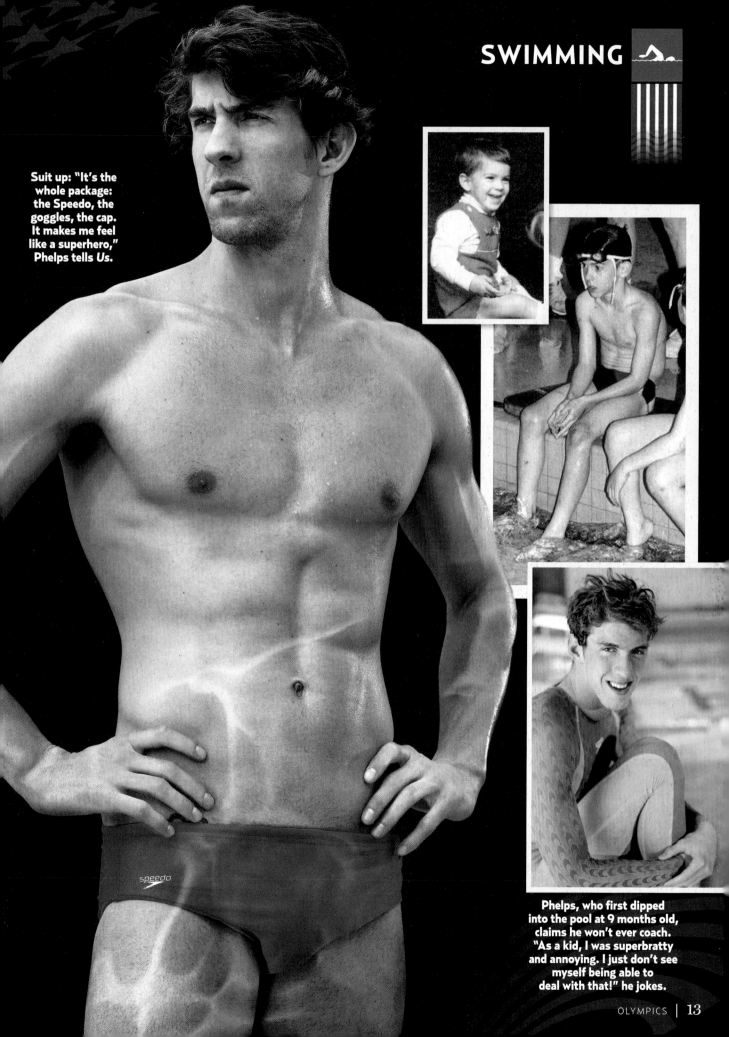

SWIMMING

Suit up: "It's the whole package: the Speedo, the goggles, the cap. It makes me feel like a superhero," Phelps tells *Us*.

Phelps, who first dipped into the pool at 9 months old, claims he won't ever coach. "As a kid, I was superbratty and annoying. I just don't see myself being able to deal with that!" he jokes.

SWIMMING

LIVING THE HIGH LIFE

After dominating 2008's Games, he hosted *Saturday Night Live* ("It was pretty great"), rubbed elbows with A-listers (like rapper Lil Wayne!) and had girls hurling themselves at him. "Winning endless medals didn't hurt at all!" he tells *Us* of the perks. But for all the fun and flirting, Phelps says he's finally ready to relax. "Once I'm done with swimming, I can actually settle down. Maybe have a relationship. Who knows!"

When he's not in swimwear, "I get pretty lazy about fashion," he admits to *Us*. "I'd rather be in a pair of sweatpants!"

"I grew up thinking that in all sports, records are always made to be broken," says the avid golfer.

Party foul: "I needed to experience mistakes on my own and learn from those."

He hit up Disney World after the 2004 and 2008 Games.

His all-time favorite sports idol? Basketball legend Michael Jordan.

He's the prince of the pool, but outside of swimming, "I'm so clumsy," he tells *Us*. "It's just bad news!"

What rivalry? "Michael's main competition is himself," coach Bowman tells *Us*.

"Standing on top of a medal podium never gets old. It's the coolest thing."

MICHAEL PHELPS

TRAINING A CHAMPION

With his 6-foot-4 frame, size 14 feet and double-jointed arms and legs, Phelps was built to swim. But it takes more than a gifted physique to win gold. "I wanted Michael to have as much training in the bank as possible," coach Bob Bowman tells *Us*. For Phelps, that meant waking up at 6:30 every morning for relentless weight training, refining his strokes in an aquatic treadmill and, every night for nearly a year, sleeping in a hyperbaric chamber that simulates high altitude, improving endurance. Says Phelps, "Bob talked me into challenging myself because I could possibly rewrite Olympic history." His secret to pushing himself through these workouts? "Listening to Skrillex and Deadmau5. They get my heart rate going!"

Bowman has coached Phelps for 16 years.

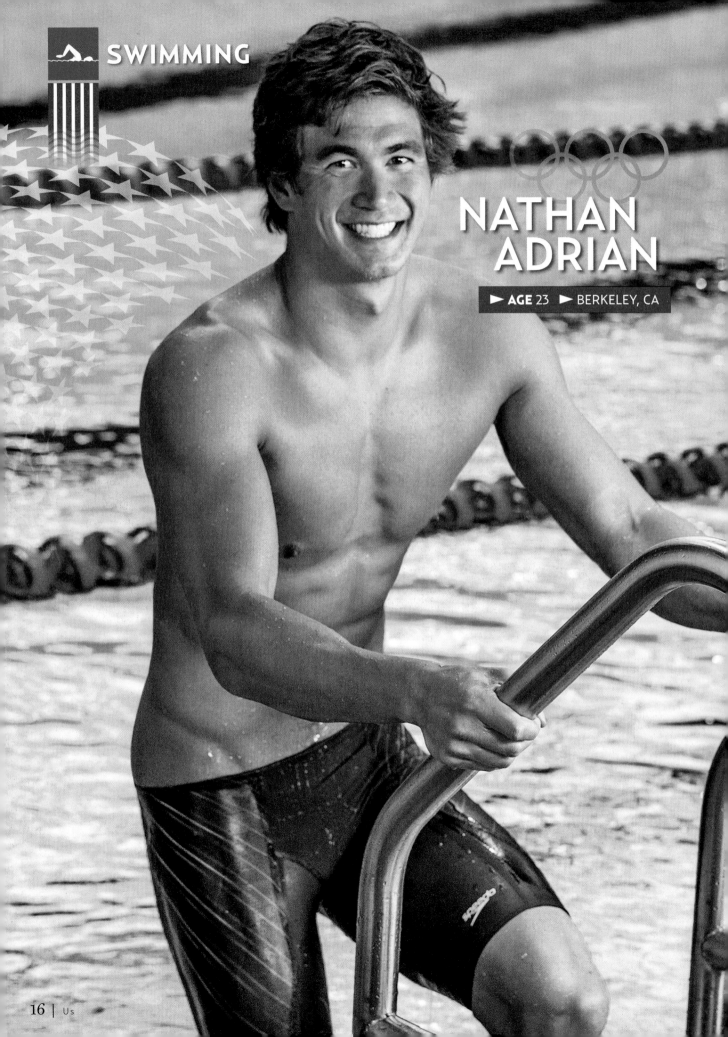

SWIMMING

NATHAN ADRIAN

► **AGE** 23 ► BERKELEY, CA

"I started taking swimming lessons at 2," says Adrian (left, with a childhood pal). "I had a ton of energy as a kid!"

H ow's this for ironic? Olympic-gold swimmer Adrian loves going to the beach — yet he's terrified of the water! "It must be a *Jaws* thing," he jokes to *Us*. "I get freaked out in the ocean, when you can't see the bottom." Back in the pool, though, he's fearless: "I don't concern myself with trying to seem confident. I just think about the preparation I've done." And outside the pool? "I have some childish hobbies," he admits, "like playing with remote-control cars and helicopters." He's young at heart romantically too: "I make girls my own cards with cardboard paper and glitter glue. It shows effort!"

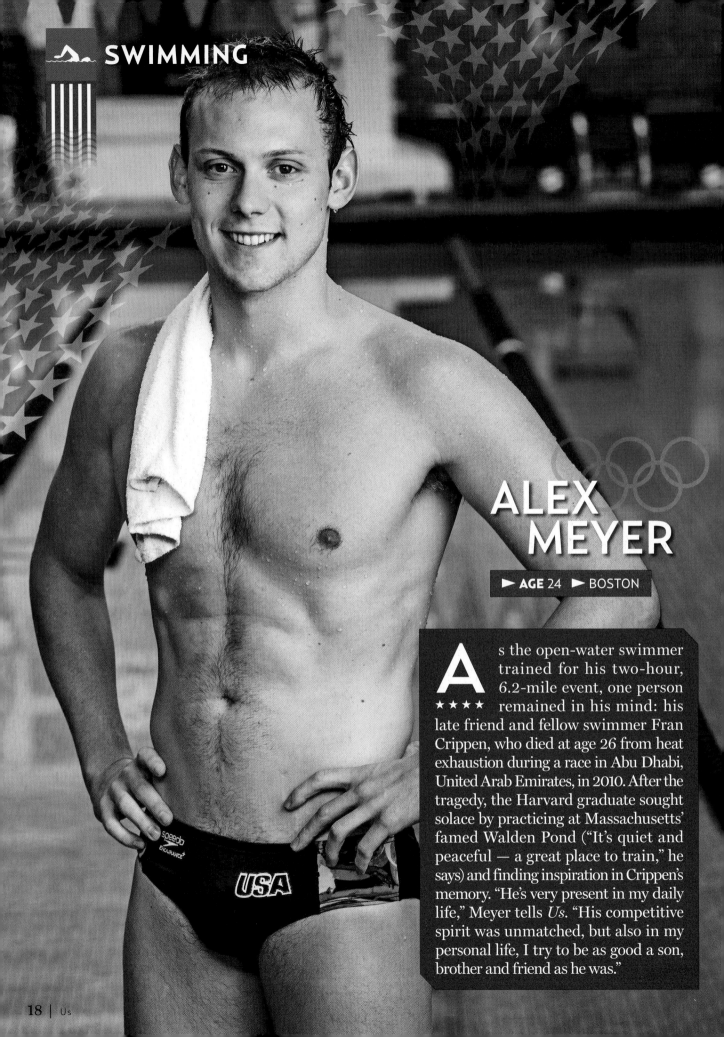

ALEX MEYER

▶ **AGE** 24 ▶ BOSTON

As the open-water swimmer trained for his two-hour, 6.2-mile event, one person ★★★★ remained in his mind: his late friend and fellow swimmer Fran Crippen, who died at age 26 from heat exhaustion during a race in Abu Dhabi, United Arab Emirates, in 2010. After the tragedy, the Harvard graduate sought solace by practicing at Massachusetts' famed Walden Pond ("It's quiet and peaceful — a great place to train," he says) and finding inspiration in Crippen's memory. "He's very present in my daily life," Meyer tells *Us*. "His competitive spirit was unmatched, but also in my personal life, I try to be as good a son, brother and friend as he was."

ERIC SHANTEAU

▶ **AGE** 28 ▶ LOS ANGELES

★ ★ ★ ★

I t's been a long road to London for the breaststroke specialist. Diagnosed with testicular cancer days before making the 2008 team, Shanteau delayed treatment to compete in Beijing. "My wife went through hell," he tells *Us* of fellow swimmer Jeri Moss, 27. But he credits his life to her: "She was the one who first sensed something was going on and pushed me to get checked out." Now three years cancer-free, "I'm calmer and more appreciative. I love the person I've become."

With wife Moss.

BRENDAN HANSEN

► **AGE** 30 ► AUSTIN

After Beijing in 2008, this four-time Olympic medalist needed a break. "I felt like life was passing me by while I stared at the bottom of the pool," Hansen tells *Us.* "I just decided to do the things I wanted to do." First order of business? Marry longtime girlfriend and sixth-grade math teacher Martha, 30, in 2010. "We traveled, bought a house, made time for the little things in life." Yet ironically, it was his wife who nudged him out of retirement. "She knows me better than I know myself! She knew I was flirting with the idea of coming back, so she said, 'Look, are you going to regret not trying again, once we're 40 and have kids?' I said yes. And she goes, 'Well, get your butt in the water, because I don't want to live with that man.' She was 100 percent behind me. After that, I was like, Game on!"

With swimmer beau of one year John Martens, 18, before junior prom. "I love dancing, especially to hip-hop!" she tells *Us*.

MISSY FRANKLIN

A Prince William fan with a Phelpsian flare for breaking records? Meet the first-time Olympian who's making a huge splash

▶ **AGE** 17 ▶ CENTENNIAL, CO

SWIMMING

Missy Franklin has it all: the looks ("I love my legs"), the smarts (a 3.95 GPA!) and the dream boyfriend ("John's incredible, and I'm so lucky"). Not to mention that, with her 6-foot-1 frame, size-13 feet and 8.5-inch hands, she boasts a killer swimmer's bod bound to break records. Another advantage? The Olympic rookie has Michael Phelps as a mentor. "I'm a little nervous, but Michael's always there for me when I need advice," says Franklin, whose dad calls her Missy the Missile. "It's flattering we're mentioned in the same sentence, though there's really no comparison."

Their biggest difference? Phelps went pro at age 16, while Franklin has refused more than $150,000 of winnings so she can still swim competitively in college. (NCAA rules prohibit students from accepting sponsorships.) "I'm lucky to have parents who support my desire to be a normal teen." Even in London, she'd rather see the sights like an ordinary girl than worry about being No. 1. "I want to ride a double-decker bus and meet One Direction, Prince William and Kate Middleton. I am in love with all of them!"

Living at home means cleaning up after the family's Alaskan malamute, Ruger. "I help with chores as much as I can."

> *"I love going to the mall and the movies. At home, I refuse to read or talk about swimming!"*
>
> MISSY FRANKLIN

"It would be easier to get homeschooled, but my friends are too important," says the Regis Jesuit High School senior. "I love going to all the football games with them."

Bookworm alert: "I absolutely love reading," she tells *Us*. "I've read the *Hunger Games* trilogy twice!"

"I started driving a year ago, and I still need to text my parents where I go," says Franklin (with physician mom D.A. and business consultant dad Richard).

NATALIE COUGHLIN

▶ **AGE** 29 ▶ VALLEJO, CA

History maker! "I already have 11 medals, so if this all ended today, I'd still be very proud," ★★★★ Coughlin tells *Us*. Yet, just two medals shy of becoming the most decorated female Olympian ever, she did feel pressure going into her third Games. "I had an idea of what was expected of me. But I knew I could swim better because I'm stronger." What else changed since 2008? She revamped her diet ("I raise my own chickens for organic eggs"), mixed up her training ("Meditating helps me feel in tip-top shape") and wed swim coach Ethan Hall, 33, in 2009. "We've been together my entire career, so he knows exactly what it takes for me to succeed."

At 10 months old, she took her first swimming lessons. By 5, she swam competitively, and she turned pro at 21. "I get to be out in the sun and travel the world. It's cool!"

GYMNASTICS BOOT CAMP

THE ROAD TO

*Inside Team USA's gymnastics training facility,
where Olympic champions are made*

OLYMPIC
NING SITE

USA
GYMNASTICS

KAROLYI'S
HALL OF FAME

GOLD

Marta
(foreground)
and Bela Karolyi
have coached
gold medalists
such as Nadia
Comaneci
and Mary
Lou Retton.

GYMNASTICS

Every month throughout their entire careers, the nation's top gymnasts ★ ★ ★ ★ report to Bela and Marta Karolyi's rural Texas ranch for four days of training and mock competitions. "It's exhausting!" senior team member Aly Raisman, 18, tells *Us* of the 8 A.M. to 7 P.M. days. And the girls aren't just pushed to their physical limits. "It's just as important to be strong mentally," says national team coordinator Marta, who, along with her husband, has taught 28 Olympians, including nine gold medalists. "You have to learn to use your nerves and adrenaline to your advantage." But it's not all work and no play: At night, in their dormlike rooms, they crash each other's bunk beds to gossip, play with iPads, watch scary movies — and cope with occasional critters. "There are tons of animals and bugs everywhere!" says Raisman. "Once, I saw a lizard next to my bed. I jumped because I was scared and my textbook fell on top of it, squishing it. It was so disgusting!"

History in the making! Students of the past (like Kerri Strug, below) and present adorn the gym walls.

Reality check! "A lot of girls are queens at their home gyms," Bela tells *Us*. "They come here and stand next to world champions."

Bela now maintains the facilities at the 2,000-acre ranch, which is equipped with three training gyms, a sauna and an Olympic-size swimming pool.

REGISTRATION

Veteran Nastia Liukin often jogs in the rural area.

"We eat at one table, the coaches and staff at another," says gymnast Gabby Douglas. "It's a lot of chicken and salmon!"

"We've been going to camp since we were little," Douglas tells *Us*. "Marta is like our mom on the national team!"

"Fight for it!" Marta tells them. "Pretend this is the world championships!"

"This is the place where friendships are built and team spirit is developed."

MARTA KAROLYI

Putting their best feet forward: "We have a choreographer who helps us work on our leaps and turns," says Douglas.

"We give 100 percent every day," Sabrina Vega tells *Us.*

Kennedy Baker and her teammates undergo thorough physical testing on the first day.

She started the sport at age 4.

After graduation next year, "I hope to go to UCLA," says Wieber (with coach John Geddert).

Wieber (at right, in glasses) with siblings Lindsay, Ryan and Kyra (from left).

The beam is only 4 inches wide, but for Wieber, "it's just like walking on the sidewalk," she says.

JORDYN WIEBER

▶ **AGE** 17 ▶ DEWITT, MI

I t ain't easy being the reigning world champ in gymnastics and (as ESPN and *Sports Illustrated* have dubbed her) the It girl of the 2012 Games. "It's tough!" the straight-A student admits to *Us*. Thanks to grueling weekday practices, "I have to catch up on a *lot* of homework on weekends. But I've had the same schedule since fifth grade, so I'm used to it." Indeed, says mom Rita, "she was pretty intense and focused as a kid. Even at age 6, she'd get upset if her ride to practice was late!" Not to say Wieber doesn't ever let her hair down. "I'm best friends with Aly Raisman and McKayla Maroney," she says of her U.S. teammates. "We text, watch TV, chitchat, stuff like that. My favorite shows are *Glee* and *Grey's Anatomy*. Oh, and I love the Kardashians!"

"She's hysterically funny," says her mom. "She's so full of life."

With older sister Joyelle, now 19.

With mom Natalie and big sis Arielle, now 23.

Gabrielle "Gabby" Douglas set her sights higher than just medal wins in London. "The ★★★★ queen's guards are so serious. I want to try and make them laugh!" says the teen, known among fans as the Flying Squirrel for her soaring uneven-bar dismounts. But jokes aside, Douglas has sacrificed much to make it this far: At 14 years old, she moved away from her native Virginia to live with a host family in Iowa in order to train with Liang Chow, coach of 2008 gold medalist Shawn Johnson. "She hasn't been home since 2010," mom Natalie Hawkins tells *Us*. "But we talk every day and we watch *Make It or Break It* [ABC Family's teen-gymnast drama] together on Skype." Admits Douglas, "It was hard being away at first. But I'm stronger because of it!"

GABBY DOUGLAS

▶ **AGE** 16 ▶ WEST DES MOINES, IA

Athletic genes! Dad Michael once played quarterback for Purdue University.

With sis Tarynn, now 6.

Before gymnastics, she did soccer, ice skating and tennis.

McKAYLA MARONEY

▶ **AGE** 16 ▶ LONG BEACH, CA

All about ambition! "Since I was 6, I dreamed about making it to the Olympics," Maroney tells *Us*. Now, thanks to eight-hour training days and a striking vault routine (which won her gold at last year's World Championships and pushed her team to No. 1!), she's become America's secret weapon. "Of course I miss out on being a normal teen," says the lifelong California girl, who opts for homeschooling. "But I still go on Facebook, hang with my friends and tan outside." Her next stop after London? Hollywood! "When I'm done with gymnastics, I want to be a TV and movie actress," she declares. "My favorite shows are *How I Met Your Mother* and *New Girl* because it's nice to just laugh after a long day. Or maybe I'll act and do gymnastics at the same time. It depends how my body feels. You never know!"

Perks of a champion? Adoring fans, TV cameos (like *Gossip Girl*!) and a killer shoe collection. "I bought my first pair of Louboutins!"

Little Liukin left Russia by age 3.

With her dad and coach, Valeri Liukin. "My medals stay in his safe!"

NASTIA LIUKIN

► **AGE** 22 ► PARKER, TX

She scored five medals in 2008 — including the gold for all-around!

I n the gymnastics gaggle of gals, "I'm a senior citizen!" the reigning gold medalist ★ ★ ★ ★ jokes to *Us*. "It's harder now to keep in shape. In Beijing, I was 18 with a body of a 15-year-old!" Which may be why, after 2008, Liukin took three years off. The reason for her comeback? "I wanted to help win a team gold medal. We were *so close* last time."

After this summer, though, she'll hang up her leotard for good. "I'm really excited to move to New York, start school and be somewhat normal." Her goals: Find an abode big enough for a longtime Texan ("I'm like, What the heck! at these New York one-bedrooms!"), get her dating life back on track (she won't confirm rumors she dated Olympic ice skater Evan Lysacek, but says, "We're still very close") and fit in with her New York University peers. "I'm going to be the oldest freshman ever," says the sports management major. "All the 18-year-olds are going to ask to borrow my ID!"

Family ties! From left: sis Chloe, 12; insurance exec dad Rick; youngest sister Madison, 10; Aly; homemaker mom Lynn; and brother Brett, 16.

"I like to help design my own leotards," says Raisman, who also does her own hair and makeup. "My coach has to OK them, but it's really fun!"

ALY RAISMAN

▶ **AGE** 18 ▶ NEEDHAM, MA

From her family home to where she trained for the Olympics, the star gymnast takes Us behind the scenes

"Little girls asking for my autograph never gets old. To make someone's day feels amazing!"

ALY RAISMAN

The athlete, who has practiced gymnastics for a decade and a half, collects all her passes from past competitions.

Bragging rights! "These aren't even half of my medals and trophies from when I was little," says Raisman. And she already has a spot reserved for Olympic awards: "It's in my room so I can be reminded of all the hard work I put in."

"I always call my parents before a meet and talk to them for a few minutes. They help me stay positive."

ALY RAISMAN

N ot your average senior year! Sure, in the last 12 months, ★★★★ Alexandra "Aly" Raisman has partied at her prom ("My jeweled dress was so elegant"); blasted Carly Rae Jepsen 24/7 with her BFFs ("'Call Me Maybe' is my *favorite* song"); turned down her fair share of boys ("I don't like the drama!"); and finally graduated high school ("There was an all-night party after"). But unlike her peers in her small New England suburban town, this teen logged 35 hours each week gearing up for her first trip to the Olympics. "I had the best of both worlds," Raisman tells *Us*. "I got to go out with my friends and have a life outside of the gym. But I was also this high school senior training for the Olympics! It was *really* cool."

Her family couldn't be more proud. "They've been so supportive and trusting of what I can do," says Raisman, who started doing splits and tumbling around at 2 years old during Mommy and Me classes. Plus, her parents and three younger siblings get to reap the perks of her success, like traveling with her to London — and, in her brother's case, getting to meet his beloved Boston Celtics. "I always joke about how I'm the one sweating, doing all the hard work, and he gets to enjoy the ride!" she says. However, going for the gold was never Raisman's only goal. After her Olympic summer, "I want to go to college away from home because I want the whole dorm experience. I want to major in business or fashion so I can create workout clothes, like cute leggings and jackets in bright colors!"

"This is my vision board with my goals." The Olympic rings: "I want to win medals!" The purple sports bra: "I'd like to design workout clothes." Taylor Swift: "I really want to meet her!"

"I bought my prom dress online. No other girl wore it!"

She finished her high school studies online to focus on training.

Are they or aren't they? Prom date Jamie McGill gave her pink roses — but she insists things are only platonic. "He's just a friend, not a boyfriend."

GYMNASTICS

BECOMING AN OLYMPIAN

Rest and relaxation? Not her style. "I don't like lying around all day," Raisman tells *Us*. So even when she's not in the gym practicing splits, "I'm stretching, going for walks or doing hot yoga." Her morning routine: "I eat a bowl of Special K and then run 10 minutes on the treadmill." For lunch, she opts for salads. "When I'm out in the mall with my friends, they'll all get huge burritos. But I don't like to feel heavy during workouts. If I want to splurge, I'll get frozen yogurt." Indeed, keeping her body strong remains her top priority. "I work hard for it, and being powerful helps when I'm tumbling on the beam or off the vault."

Guys think twice before making a move in front of her brother. "Even though he's younger, he's very protective."

Her favorite gymnastics event? The floor exercise.

The self-proclaimed shopaholic often hits up Victoria's Secret, Ralph Lauren and Bloomingdale's.

She likes to clip photos of her family and closest pals for collages. "Saturday nights are when I'll hang out at a friend's house."

"I have two Malteses: Magic and Coco. They both bark a lot!"

What a great hostess! "My mom cooks, and I like to serve people who come over."

"I like to keep my makeup natural: a little pink lip gloss and some eyeliner."

ALY RAISMAN

"I *really* like Tyler Seguin from the Boston Bruins," the ice hockey fan tells *Us* of her crush.

Worth the gold! "Being a gymnast in the Bronx was rough at times. Kids didn't understand my passion."

With his teacher and mom, Damaris. "It feels good to make my parents proud."

JOHN OROZCO

► **AGE** 19 ► COLORADO SPRINGS, CO

All it took was a pamphlet for his dreams to change. The Bronx native's dad, William, a sanitation supervisor, "came home from work one day with flyers for free gymnastics tryouts," the 5-foot-4 athlete tells *Us*. "I was into martial arts at the time, but I tried a class, and the moment I stepped on the floor and started flipping around, I didn't want to stop." Though he went on to earn a black belt, the single star still craved more acrobatic challenges. "I just liked mastering all gymnastics' different skills." And the Olympic newcomer isn't one to let others tease him about his sport. "People say, 'Oh, do you twirl around?' I'm like, 'No, but can you do a double backflip with a double twist?' That's my argument!"

Behind every strong man is an even stronger woman. That's certainly the case for this ★ ★ ★ ★ Olympian, who said "I do" to University of Texas med student Haley DeProspero, 24, the year after he won silver in 2008. "She's my backbone," he gushes to *Us*. "We get each other because she used to be a gymnast too. She understands the time and effort I put into what I'm doing." Indeed, training for London meant the 5-foot-1 star had to spend six hours each day at practice. (His specialty: an unmatched high bar routine.) And when he needed to let off steam outside of the gym? "I'd ride motorcycles all the time with my teammates," Horton says. "I have two myself: a Honda Cruiser and a Suzuki."

JONATHAN HORTON

► **AGE** 26 ► HOUSTON

"We met at orientation at the University of Oklahoma and have been together ever since!"

DANELL LEYVA

► AGE 20   ► MIAMI

A former gymnast for Team Cuba, Leyva's mom, Maria Gonzalez, held high standards for her son from day one. "When I was a kid, I wanted to become a gymnast, but my mom said my arms were too long, my butt too big and my feet too flat!" he tells *Us*. But he won her over with the help of stepdad (and lifelong coach) Yin Alvarez. "I watched videos, took classes and showed that I had heart and determination. I'm always trying to prove people wrong by being the best!" Still, the Olympic first-timer has a lot to prove, like whether he can beat his rival, Horton. "My parents get much more nervous than I do, but that energizes me during routines."

TRACK & FIELD

BRYAN CLAY

Another amazing race! The defending gold-medalist decathlete opens up about being a top jock and a No. 1 dad

▶ **AGE** 32   ▶ GLENDORA, CA

On his Wheaties cereal box, he's dubbed the World's Greatest Athlete. And no wonder: Bryan Clay excels in not one but 10 grueling ★ ★ ★ ★ events, from javelin to shotput and hurdles. Fortunately, "this is my third Olympics, so it's less nerve-wracking," he tells *Us*. "I'm just enjoying it!" Keeping him grounded? Homemaker wife Sarah, 33, and kids Jacob, 7, Kate, 5, and Ellie, 2. "They visit Daddy at the track, bring Jamba Juice and play on the grass. They don't know how cool my job is!" Still, his youngest does love when he brings home gold. "Sometimes I'll find Ellie wearing my Beijing medal around the house!"

"My wife is an amazing partner and the perfect mom," he says of college sweetheart Sarah (holding daughter Ellie). "She walks our kids to school and cooks all of our meals — except for barbecue. That's when I take over!"

"I'm big on family. I'll spend extra money to fly my wife and kids out to where I am."

BRYAN CLAY

"I wake up at 6 A.M. to train, but I'm home by 3:30 P.M. so I can play in the pool or ride bikes with my kids," says Clay. His 2008 Wheaties box is in a display case in his home office (inset).

Where does he keep his medals? "Usually in a sock drawer or a junk drawer in the kitchen," he jokes.

From left: "Ellie is the athlete, always active and loves to swim. Jacob is the brain, very analytical. And Kate is a girlie-girl who loves her princess dresses," says Clay.

Clay typically hits the gym for two hours of weight training every morning. Also crucial to his A.M. routine: "Coffee, and a quick devotional with my wife at home."

His one travel must: a scrapbook made by his wife, packed with inspirational Bible verses and "I love you" notes from the kids. "I just tear up flipping through it," he tells Us.

"I grew up in Hawaii, so I listen to Hawaiian music a lot," he says. "Also, my faith is a big part of my life, so I like worship music."

A gold medal for grooming! Before each competition, says Clay, "I always cut my hair. I don't know why. It's just something that I started doing!"

"The lucky thing about training seven hours a day is I can eat whatever I want!"

BRYAN CLAY

How does he like to celebrate a win? "I sleep in and eat a huge breakfast!" Hardee tells *Us*.

TREY HARDEE

► **AGE** 28   ► AUSTIN

Meet the man giving Bryan Clay a run for his money. "I don't want to say I'm invincible, but I've become resistant to sickness, injury and any kind of obstacle," the decathlete brags to *Us*. Indeed, the Olympic rookie competes hard against U.S. rivals Clay and Ashton Eaton — and boasts two World Championship gold medals to prove it. "But when the competition is over, we become brothers because the decathlon is such a torturous experience!" jokes the 6-foot-5 star. Another source of support: girlfriend of three years Chelsea Johnson, 28. "She recently retired from pole vaulting, so she understands what I do. It's way easier dating another athlete."

LASHINDA DEMUS

► **AGE** 29 ► PALMDALE, CA

"My twins always cheer loud enough for me to hear before I get on the blocks!" she says.

Career vs. family. Many women athletes assume they need to choose, just like history's third fastest female hurdler. "I was starting my career when I had twins," says Demus, mom to Dontay and Duaine, 5. (Dad is husband-agent Jamel Mayrant, 28.) "I didn't want to be pregnant. It was overwhelming for me, a lot of dark emotions. I thought about abortion. But when I saw the sonogram, it triggered something inside me: Wait, why can't I have kids *and* a career? I'll be fine. I'll be back. I'll be good again." Having crossed her greatest hurdle, she now embraces the challenges of being an Olympic mom. "We don't have a nanny!" she says. "I don't want to miss any part of them growing up."

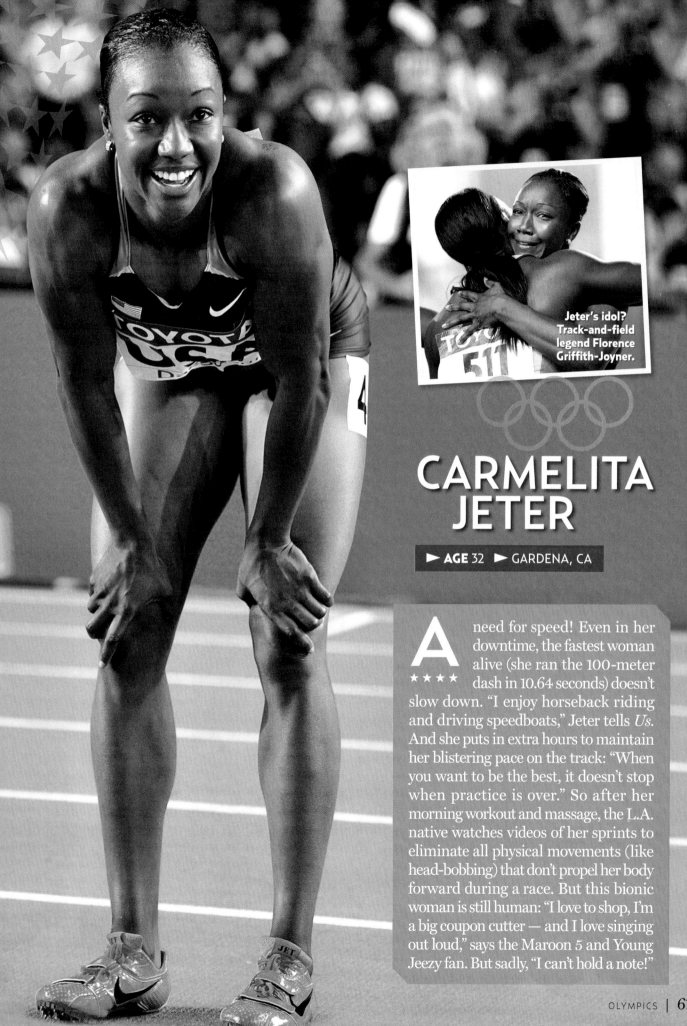

Jeter's idol? Track-and-field legend Florence Griffith-Joyner.

CARMELITA JETER

► **AGE** 32 ► GARDENA, CA

A need for speed! Even in her downtime, the fastest woman alive (she ran the 100-meter dash in 10.64 seconds) doesn't slow down. "I enjoy horseback riding and driving speedboats," Jeter tells *Us*. And she puts in extra hours to maintain her blistering pace on the track: "When you want to be the best, it doesn't stop when practice is over." So after her morning workout and massage, the L.A. native watches videos of her sprints to eliminate all physical movements (like head-bobbing) that don't propel her body forward during a race. But this bionic woman is still human: "I love to shop, I'm a big coupon cutter — and I love singing out loud," says the Maroon 5 and Young Jeezy fan. But sadly, "I can't hold a note!"

With fiancée Theisen.

ASHTON EATON

▶ **AGE** 24 ▶ EUGENE, OR

The bar has always been set high for Eaton. "That's how I learned to achieve," says the decathlete, who credits his drive to single mom Roslyn. Indeed, for his very first race in fourth grade, she bought him a uniform *and* special racing shoes. "She could have said, 'Ashton, honestly, it's a PE class. Big deal,'" says Eaton. "But no, she went and bought me spikes!" Clearly, Mom saw talent: By fifth grade, he ran cross-country with the high school team. Fast-forward to 2012: "My fiancée and I train together every day," he tells *Us* of Brianne Theisen, 23, who represents Canada in the heptathlon. "She motivates me. I used to stay up late with friends or playing video games, but because of her, now I go to bed at 10 to get a good sleep for the next day!"

DECATHLON 411

This year, thanks to Clay, Hardee and Eaton, the U.S. reigns supreme in the decathlon. Derived from the ancient Greek pentathlon, the event consists of three races, hurdles, discus, javelin, shot put, pole vault, and high and long jumps.

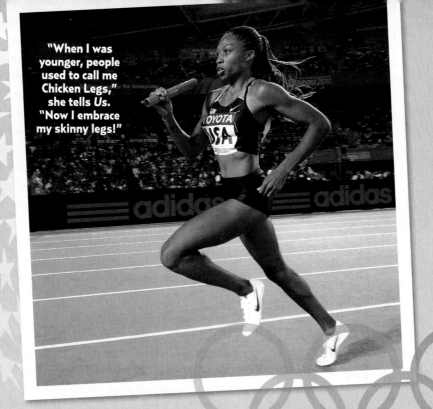

"When I was younger, people used to call me Chicken Legs," she tells *Us*. "Now I embrace my skinny legs!"

ALLYSON FELIX

Dashing diva! The stunning sprinter tells Us *about America's fierce rivalry with Jamaica — and how she cools down at home*

▶ **AGE** 26 ▶ LOS ANGELES

There's never been a bigger race in track-and-field history than USA vs. Jamaica. And this year, America's biggest sprinting star refuses to settle for silver. "Being second to [Jamaica's] Veronica Campbell-Brown in 2004 and 2008 has been my biggest motivation," Olympic veteran Felix tells *Us*. "I enjoy our rivalry. I run better when I'm up against her." Cheering from the bleachers? Minister dad Paul, schoolteacher mom Marlean and brother Wes, 29, who's also her agent. But even when family can't make it to her meets, she always wears a keepsake: "A cross necklace that my mom gave me in 2004. It calms my nerves and reminds me that running is my gift from God."

Fit to win! "I'll spend two hours in the gym working on my core." And when she's craving a snack? "I treat myself to frozen grapes."

Felix lives in a two-bedroom L.A. pad with her 4-year-old Yorkie, Chloe. "My mom watches her when I'm not at home."

Top chef! "I bake a really great German chocolate cake for my teammates," she tells Us.

"I have about 100 pairs of tennis shoes," she says. "I like a lot of neon for summer!"

"I'm super-competitive in everything — even with hula hoops and board games!"

ALLYSON FELIX

When life gets too stressful, "I go to my parents' house, which is 30 minutes away in the suburbs," says Felix (with mom Marlean).

She unwinds by pedaling to the beach. "Playa del Rey is five minutes away, so it's relaxing to bike and enjoy the scenery."

The relationship between volleyball partners can be much like a marriage. Just ask these two Orange County beach babes. "I spend more time with Jen than anyone else — more than my own husband!" jokes Ross, who wed fellow volleyball player Brad Keenan, 30, in 2010. But she and Kessy (who's dating French volleyball pro Andy Cès, 30) didn't always get along. "We met as students at the University of Southern California," Ross tells *Us*. "My team was playing against hers, and she yelled at me on the court! I was like, This girl is a total *B*." But after they paired up professionally in 2007, "I realized I was completely wrong about her." Now, the star duo bond over contraband croissant-and-Nutella snacks ("You've gotta live a little!" says Kessy), shopping for swimsuits (key criterion: must be wedgieproof) and hair issues. "It's hard when you're out in the sun," Kessy says. "I try not to shampoo or brush too much. We'll put in product, scrunch-dry it and get a nice wavy beach look!"

APRIL
ROSS

► **AGE** 30 ► NEWPORT BEACH, CA

JENNIFER
KESSY

► **AGE** 35 ► SAN CLEMENTE, CA

VOLLEYBALL

KERRI WALSH

▶ **AGE** 33 ▶ HERMOSA BEACH, CA

This two-time Olympic champ refuses to take her eye off the gold. But she's not exactly ★ ★ ★ talking about another medal. "When my wedding band slipped off into the sand at the 2008 Games, I never though I'd get it back!" says Walsh, who wed volleyball pro Casey Jennings, 37, in 2005. "I've packed a clear rubber ring to wear over it ever since." She also always travels with sons Joey, 3, and Sundance, 2. "When they're not with me, my chest gets tight, and I stop eating and sleeping. I put them in these Team USA diapers from Pampers that are so dang cute. They're very patriotic!"

Think she has her hands full now? "I want to get pregnant again right after London!"

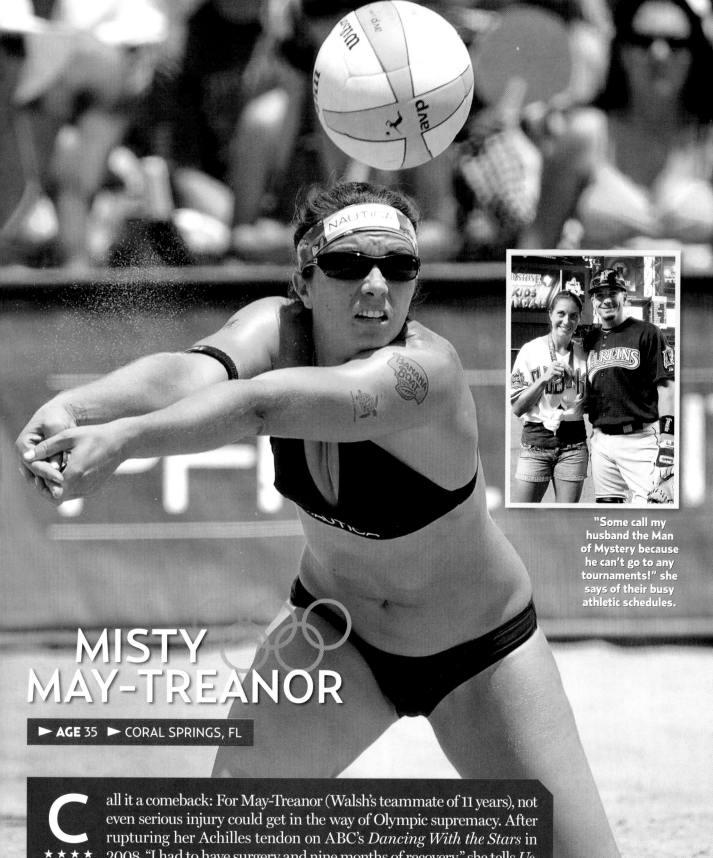

"Some call my husband the Man of Mystery because he can't go to any tournaments!" she says of their busy athletic schedules.

MISTY MAY-TREANOR

► **AGE** 35 ► CORAL SPRINGS, FL

C
★ ★ ★ ★
all it a comeback: For May-Treanor (Walsh's teammate of 11 years), not even serious injury could get in the way of Olympic supremacy. After rupturing her Achilles tendon on ABC's *Dancing With the Stars* in 2008, "I had to have surgery and nine months of recovery," she tells *Us*. "I'd never been injured before. I just hopped back doing the jive and heard a pop! But I wasn't worried. I knew I'd come back stronger." That she did. By 2010, the star (married to L.A. Dodgers catcher Matt Treanor, 36) hit the court again — and upped her record to 107 tournament wins. "You don't know why certain things happen, but they do. As they say in show business, the show must go on!"

BETSEY ARMSTRONG
▶ **AGE** 29 ▶ LONG BEACH, CA

BRENDA VILLA
▶ **AGE** 32 ▶ LONG BEACH, CA

MERRILL MOSES

▶ **AGE** 34 ▶ RANCHO PALOS VERDES, CA

TONY AZEVEDO

▶ **AGE** 30 ▶ THOUSAND OAKS, CA

People assume that water polo is brutal, nasty and intense — and it absolutely is!" two-time Olympic goalkeeper Armstrong tells *Us*. Think: a solid hour of treading water while kicking, punching, biting, ★ ★ ★ ★ scratching — and even attempting to tear off opponents' swimsuits. Not surprisingly, the Team USA players prefer a calmer lifestyle out of the pool. "We get coffee as a team and relax before games," Armstrong says of the women's team. And they swear by yoga: "It helps open your legs for treading." As for the men? They chill with soft music: "I like Jack Johnson," says Moses. And confesses team captain Tony Azevedo, "I love celebrity magazines! At the airport, the guys always look at me. A four-time Olympian, sitting there reading *Us Weekly*."

TAE KWON DO

STEVEN
LOPEZ

► AGE 33 ► SUGAR LAND, TX

DIANA LOPEZ

▶ **AGE** 28 ▶ SUGAR LAND, TX

Introducing the first family of tae kwon do! The Lopez siblings — who have brought home medals from every Olympiad since 2000 — owe their dominance of the sport to dad Julio. A fan of kung fu flicks, he first enrolled eldest son Jean (now 38) in a martial-arts class — and his other kids, Steven, Diana and Mark (now 30), quickly followed suit. "We'd get in our Chevy Astro, drive an hour away and pay $100 for a one-hour lesson," Steven tells *Us*. "It was tough but fun!" Now Jean's the family coach, while mom Ondina plays cheerleader. "She's hard-core!" says Steven. (Fun fact: Steven was asked to be ABC's Bachelor after the 2004 Games, but he declined.) "My mom will say, 'Don't even let 'em make it into the ring with you.'" Seconds Diana, "She's, like, shadowboxing on the side. *She* was the one who always pressured me to be tougher, not my brothers!" Mom's plea? Guilty as charged. Jokes Ondina to *Us*, "They'll tell me, 'Relax, Mama. Relax!'"

"I had to first learn how to walk in heels!" she says of her 2011 stint on ABC's *Dancing With the Stars.*

HOPE SOLO

▶ **AGE** 31 ▶ SEATTLE

S he's been called soccer's biggest sex symbol. Yet despite gracing the covers of *Vogue*, *Sports Illustrated* and *ESPN* (sans clothes!), the U.S. team's goalkeeper grew up with major self-esteem problems: "I felt insecure ★★★★ about my build. I didn't feel very feminine." To cope, Solo threw herself into soccer, a passion shared with her late father, Jeffrey, an intermittently homeless Vietnam vet. "We'd talk for hours and hours about sports," says Solo, who sprinkled his ashes in the goal box before every World Cup game after his death of heart failure in 2007. "He understood life and sports, and that's why he knew me so well."

ERROL SPENCE

▶ **AGE** 22 ▶ DESOTO, TX

Boxing has been a part of Spence's life for as long as he can remember. "My dad was a big Lennox Lewis fan, so we would watch his fights at the local barbershop when I was a kid," he tells *Us*. But it wasn't until age 15 when he put on his own gloves. "I began boxing just to stay busy one summer," he says. "Two months later, I was boxing competitively." Now with three national championship titles under his belt, the welterweight works around the clock — even running at 2 A.M. to avoid the Texas heat. That's not to say he's immune to prefight jitters. "I do get butter-flies," he admits. "But as soon as that bell rings, watch out!"

BOXING

JOSEPH DIAZ JR.

▶ **AGE** 19 ▶ SOUTH EL MONTE, CA

F ather knows best! "My dad got me into boxing," Diaz tells *Us*. "He wanted me to ★★★★ learn self-defense because I was bullied for being small. I was so excited!" The 5-foot-5 athlete, who goes by JoJo, wasn't the only one who loved learning to dodge and weave. Dad Joseph Sr. picked up every training book he could find and studied hours of YouTube boxing videos. Now JoJo couldn't be happier to call his dad coach (though he has an official Olympic trainer too). "People assume we butt heads, but he's my best friend!" says the bantamweight. He even held a car wash to raise money so Dad could fly to London and root for him ringside. Says Diaz, "He's my inspiration, and he helps me with everything. I love him."

With his dad in 2007. "We're together 24/7," says Diaz.

JENNIFER NICHOLS

► **AGE** 28 ► CHEYENNE, WY

It's not easy hitting that bull's-eye! This three-time Olympian knows firsthand — and watched in awe as Jennifer Lawrence nailed her targets in *The Hunger Games*. "She did an awesome job!" Nichols gushes to *Us*. "You could tell she had professional training from her draw and her stance. Plus, it's exciting how we've seen an explosion of interest in my sport!" And like her onscreen counterpart, Nichols (who began training at age 12) hates rushing romance. "I made a commitment to save my first kiss for the man I knew I was going to marry," says the devout Christian, who will wed Texas A&M University sweetheart Chris Hardy, 25, this fall in a rural farm ceremony. "Chris and I kissed when I was 27. I knew he was The One!"

DIVING

NICK McCRORY

▶ **AGE** 20 ▶ DURHAM, NC

C ★★★★ hief nutritionist on this Duke University junior's coaching team? His mom, Ana! "I live at home, so she always cooks me dinner after practice: chicken or a lean protein that's good for recovery," says McCrory, who's been dating fellow Duke swimmer Emily Kintz for three years. Another key partner: synchronized diving teammate Boudia (*right;* both also compete individually). "We train really hard! But even when there aren't competitions, I'll go up to see him at Purdue University [in Indiana] or he'll come down to see me at Duke. We spend a lot of time together!"

DAVID BOUDIA

▶ **AGE** 23 ▶ WEST LAFAYETTE, IN

Purdue senior Boudia has long dreamed of glory at the Games. "I've wanted to be an Olympian since I was 7!" the 16-time national champion tells *Us*. At first, he pursued gymnastics — but, after growing bored, switched to diving in middle school. Just one small problem: "I was petrified of heights! It's been a huge struggle my whole career." Fortunately, the athlete (who's dating fellow Purdue student Sonnie Brand) overcame his fears after working with a sports psychologist. "It came to a point where I was like, I can let this defeat me, or I can accomplish my dreams."

DIVING

TROY DUMAIS

▶ **AGE** 32 ▶ AUSTIN

Diving veteran Dumais boasts one heck of a résumé: 35 national titles, five World Championship medals and three prior trips to the Olympics. "They call me Grandpa," he jokes of his younger teammates. Still, he shows no signs of slowing down: "I train six days a week: two and a half hours in the pool, two and a half hours of weights, and then, that night, if I feel I haven't done enough, I'll do another 30 minutes at the gym." But don't mistake Dumais for a tough guy. "My cats, Tiger and Squeak, motivate me! They're just amazing. They've been with me since 2000 and have carried me through every Olympics. These boys make me feel loved."

THOMAS FINCHUM

▶ **AGE** 22 ▶ INDIANAPOLIS

Guess who trained this Olympian to dive? "My grandma! She used to be a ★ ★ ★ ★ diver. We were on a houseboat when I was 9, and she taught me to dive off of the top of it. Later, my mom signed me up for lessons." Nowadays, he trains not just at the pool but at a ballet studio. "It's about the acrobatic beauty, skill and core control." Well, one fan has already taken notice: his celeb crush, Taylor Swift. "I met her in 2008 at one of her concerts. She was like, 'I watched you in the Olympics! You're my favorite diver.' I, like, freaked out!"

MOST MEMORABLE MOMENTS

Heart-stopping! From record-setting triumphs to tragic falls from grace, Us revisits a few of the Olympic Games' biggest nail-biters

▶ **1988** SEOUL, SOUTH KOREA

THE FASTEST WOMAN ON EARTH
FLORENCE GRIFFITH-JOYNER

Just 10.62 seconds. That's how long it took history's most legendary track-and-field star to dash 100 meters in 1988, setting a world record that remains ★ ★ ★ unbroken to this day. As if that weren't enough, five days later, FloJo — the seventh of 11 children, who grew up in an L.A. housing project — set *another* still-unchallenged record of 200 meters in 21.34 seconds. "Don't try to be like me," she later told fans of her role-model status, before succumbing to epilepsy in 1998 at age 38. "Be *better* than me."

"I've always been attracted to long nails!" she said of her signature 6-inch manicure. But she trimmed them for relay races to grab the baton more easily.

► **1996** ATLANTA

THE UNBREAKABLE SPIRIT
KERRI STRUG

Q uitting just wasn't an option.
Locked in battle with Russia,
the U.S. women's gymnastics
★ ★ ★ ★ team pinned their hopes of
winning America's first-ever team gold
on Strug's vault exercise. But the 18-year-
old stumbled upon landing, tearing
two ligaments in her left ankle. After
huddling with coach Bela Karolyi, she
decided to go again. "This is what you
dream about from when you're 5 years
old," she said later. "I wasn't going to
stop!" Indeed, she nailed her do-over
with a gold-worthy 9.7 score — bursting
into tears of joy and pain. "In my 35
years of coaching I have never seen
such a moment," said Karolyi. "People
think these girls are fragile dolls.
They're not. They're courageous."

Strug (with
Karolyi) delayed
a hospital visit
to join the
team's medal
ceremony.

LITTLE MISS PERFECT 10
MARY LOU RETTON

N ★★★★ o American woman had ever won first place in gymnastics — until this 16-year-old West Virginian rocked the crowds at the 1984 Games. After near-flawless performances on the balance beam and uneven bars, and a 10.0 score on her floor routine, Retton needed one last perfect 10 on the vault to win the women's all-around competition. (Even the slightest wobble in her landing would relegate her to second place.) She nailed it — earning America's first gymnastics gold medal and prompting coach Karolyi to leap over the barriers with joy. "He starts chanting, 'Ten! Ten!' The whole arena is going, 'Ten! Ten!'" Retton recalls. "It's hard to describe in words the overwhelming sense of pride!"

Retton had knee surgery just six weeks before. "I knew it was going to be a dogfight, but I was up for it," she says. "Nothing was going to stop me."

THE DREAM TEAM

M
★★★★
ichael Jordan. Magic Johnson. Larry Bird. Charles Barkley. The roster for the 1992 U.S. men's basketball team — the first-ever to allow pro players — read like a who's who of the biggest NBA stars of all time. But in donning their Team USA jerseys, the Olympians left their egos at home. "Nobody cared whose name was in the paper," recalls Johnson, the team captain. "All we cared about was winning the game and dominating." And dominate they did — crushing every challenger by an average of 44 points and steamrolling their way to gold. As Cuba's team coach lamented, "You can't cover the sun with your finger."

Lords of the rings (from left): Bird, Jordan, Scottie Pippen and Johnson. "It was like Elvis and the Beatles put together," remembers U.S. coach Chuck Daly. "Traveling with the Dream Team was like traveling with 12 rock stars. That's all I can compare it to."

Louganis finished his dives 35 minutes after receiving temporary sutures — and went on to win a gold medal the very next day.

► **1988** SEOUL, SOUTH KOREA

A DIVE GONE WRONG
GREG LOUGANIS

"I think my pride was hurt more than anything else," he said of his head injury.

R enowned as the greatest diver to have lived, Louganis sent gasps through the crowd — and around the world — after gashing his head ★ ★ ★ ★ on a diving board during an extraordinarily difficult reverse two-and-a-half pike dive in Seoul. The four-time gold medalist shocked fans further in 1995 after revealing he'd been HIV positive at the time. Yet despite the ensuing controversy (physicians later concluded the transmission risk was negligible due to chlorine and dilution), "I have no regrets," he said, declaring, "I wanted my story to motivate those people who are HIV positive . . . to understand life isn't over yet."